BIBLE
DOCTRINES

◆

– Part 2 –

R. E.
HARLOW

LUKE 24:27

Developed as a study course by Emmaus Correspondence School, founded in 1942.

Many Bible study courses may also be taken via smart phones, tablets, and computers. For more information, visit the ECS website www.ecsministries.org.

Bible Doctrines — Part 2
R. E. Harlow

Published by:
Emmaus Correspondence School
(A division of ECS Ministries)
P.O. Box 1028
Dubuque, IA 52004-1028
phone: (563) 585-2070
email: ecsorders@ecsministries.org
website: www.ecsministries.org

First Edition 2016 (AK '16), 2 Units
Reprinted 2019 (AK '16), 2 Units

ISBN 978-1-59387-241-0

Code: BD2

Printed in the United States of America

STUDENT INSTRUCTIONS

"All Scripture . . . is profitable for doctrine . . ." (2 Timothy 3:16). This 2-part course will guide you through a topical study of the major teachings (doctrines) of Scripture, referencing many pertinent verses and passages relating to each doctrine. With an open Bible and an open heart, you will indeed profit from learning what the Scripture teaches about itself, God, Jesus Christ, and the Holy Spirit in Part 1, and angels, man, sin, salvation, the church, and future events in Part 2.

LESSONS YOU WILL STUDY

1. Angelology 5
2. Anthropology 13
3. Hamartiology 19
4. Soteriology – Part 1 25
5. Soteriology – Part 2 33
6. Ecclesiology – Part 1 41
7. Ecclesiology – Part 2 47
8. Eschatology 53

Note: *Bible Doctrines – Part 1* covers Bibliology, Theology Proper, Christology, and Pneumatology.

Course Components

This course has two parts: this study course and the exam booklet.

How To Study

This study has eight chapters, and each chapter has its own exam. Begin by asking God to help you understand the material. Read the chapter through at least twice, once to get a general idea of its contents and then again, slowly, looking up any Bible references given.

Begin studying immediately, or if you are in a group, as soon as the group begins. We suggest that you keep a regular schedule by trying to complete at least one chapter per week.

Exams

In the exam booklet there is one exam for each chapter (exam 1 covers chapter 1 of the course). Do not answer the questions by what you think or have always believed. The questions are designed to find out if you understand the material given in the course.

After you have completed each chapter, review the related exam and see how well you know the answers. If you find that you are having difficulty answering the questions, review the material until you think you can answer the questions. It is important that you read the Bible passages referenced as some questions may be based on the Bible text.

How Your Exams Are Graded

Your instructor will mark any incorrectly answered questions. You will be referred back to the place in the course where the correct answer is to be found. After finishing this course with a passing average, you will be awarded a certificate.

If you enrolled in a class, submit your exam papers to the leader or secretary of the class who will send them for the entire group to the Correspondence School.

See the back of the exam booklet for more information on returning the exams for grading.

1

ANGELOLOGY: THE STUDY OF ANGELS

The word *angel* itself simply means "messenger," in both the Old and New Testaments. It has a specialized usage for the created spirit-beings who serve either God or Satan. This is how we will use the term here.

The Origin of the Angels

Where did the angels come from? What are they like? What are the different kinds of angels? God created the angels. John tells in John 1:3 that "all things were made by Him [the Word, the Son of God, Christ]." Paul is still more explicit: "For by Him [Christ] were all things created that are in heaven and that are on earth, visible and invisible, whether thrones or dominions or principalities or powers. All things were created through Him and for Him" (Col. 1:16).

We know that God created all angels before He created the heavens and the earth or man, since the angels were there at the creation (see Job 38:7). As far as we know, God has never created more angels, nor do angels reproduce as humans do (see Mark 12:25). They were created individually and evidently all at the same time. Until the fall of Lucifer, "the anointed cherub," all the angels were basically similar, at least in holiness and obedience to God's will. When Lucifer fell, many angels followed him in his rebellion, though myriads remained loyal to God. These latter angels are the "unfallen" angels.

Who the Holy Angels Are

What are the angels like who resisted the temptation to follow Lucifer? Human reason and experience can tell us nothing of these things; it is only by God's revelation in the Bible that we know what angelic beings are and what they do. Angels are called "spirits" (Heb. 1:7, 14), and good angels are called "holy" (Mark 8:38). They do not have corporeal bodies and are usually invisible to human beings. "A spirit does not have flesh and bones" (Luke 24:39). Sometimes, however, angels have appeared to people in human form (Gen. 19:1, 5; Heb. 13:2). Angels are greater in power and might than humans. In rank, man was made a little lower than the angels (Ps. 8:5). From Hebrews 2:9 it appears that angels are immortal—that is, they cannot die as humans can. Angels, then, are personal spirits, created sinless by God for the purpose of serving Him.

> It is only by God's revelation in the Bible that we know what angelic beings are and what they do.

Angels are referred to hundreds of times in both the Old and New Testaments. Various words are used for categories of angels. The *archangel,* or chief angel, is named Michael (Dan. 10:21; Jude 9). His ministry was especially to Israel. The only other good angel who is named in Scripture is Gabriel (Dan. 8:16; Luke 1:19, 26). The *seraphim,* or "burning ones," are mentioned only in Isaiah 6, where they are described as guardians of the holy throne of God. The first mention of the *cherubim* is in Genesis 3:24, guarding the way to the tree of life. Their work is thus particularly associated with the holiness of God. Images of cherubim are seen in the tabernacle (Ex. 25:18), the temple of Solomon (1 Kings 6:23), and the temple of Ezekiel (Ezek. 41:18). Neither the seraphim nor the cherubim are specifically called angels, but they are generally taken to be such.

In the Old Testament we read the phrase *Angel of Jehovah* ("Angel of the LORD"; the word "LORD" in all capitals in our English Bibles always stands for the personal name of God, Jehovah, or Yahweh). In some of the passages where the phrase occurs, it is clear that the Angel or "Messenger" in question is divine (e.g. Gen. 16:11, 13; Ex. 3:2, 4). A careful study of all the passages in question will reveal that the Angel of Jehovah is the Lord Jesus Christ in pre-incarnate *theophanies,* or visible manifestations of Deity. As the Revelation of God (John 1:18), it is fitting that the Second Person of the Trinity should be the One to reveal God in the Old Testament also. How wonderful, that the One who in the incarnation was pleased to take the form of a servant was, before His incarnation, pleased to act as "the Messenger of the LORD."

The good angels, confirmed in holiness by resisting Lucifer's call to follow him, are now the ministers (servants) of God and His people (Ps. 103:20-21). Like men, angels have intellect (2 Samuel 14:20; compare 1 Peter 1:12 and Exodus 25:22), sensibility (Mark 8:38; Luke 15:10), and will (Isaiah 14:13-14—of Lucifer). Because of these characteristics, and also their strength (Ps. 103:20) and great number (Matt. 18:10; Rev. 5:11-12), they are able to help men as God directs.

What the Holy Angels Do

With reference to Christ, angels have had a widespread ministry. At the creation they praised Christ (compare Job 38:4-7 and John 1:3). They predicted the births of John the Baptist (Luke 1:17) and the Lord Jesus (Luke 1:30-38), and they announced Christ's birth to the shepherds (Luke 2:10-12). After Christ's temptation they ministered to Him (Mark 1:13; Matt. 4:11), and in Gethsemane they strengthened Him (Luke 22:43) and were ready to defend Him (Matt. 26:53). At the resurrection they rolled away the stone to let the witnesses enter the empty tomb (Christ was already risen, Matt. 28:2-4). They guarded the evidence of the resurrection (John 20:12-13) and announced the resurrection (Luke 24:4-7) to Jesus' followers. In Acts 1:10-11, angels predicted the second coming in similar fashion to the going of Christ by ascension. Now, during Christ's present session at God's right hand, the good angels take an interest in the gospel and rejoice in the salvation of sinners (1 Pet. 1:12; Luke 15:10). They will be prominent at Christ's coming to reign and to judge (Matt. 13:39, 41-42, 49-50; 2 Thess. 1:7-10, etc.). The book of Revelation contains many instances of angels administering divine judgment.

Beside worshiping and serving God, angels serve individuals and nations. Michael is the special defender of Israel (Dan. 12:1) and will regather that nation at the second coming (Matt. 24:31). The Old Testament is full of examples of angel ministrations, especially Daniel. The book of Acts has many instances of angels revealing, delivering, and guiding the early Christians (e.g. 1:9-11; 5:19-20; 8:26-29; 10:3-6; 12:7-10). Today, according to Hebrews 1:14, they are serving Christians. They desire to observe the God-ordained order of the local church (1 Cor. 11:10; 1 Tim. 5:21) and are the guardians of children (Matt. 18:10).

In view of the important work of the holy angels, Christians should speak respectfully of them and to take their existence seriously. Neither the extreme of worshiping angels (Col. 2:18) nor a flippant joking or unbelieving attitude regarding these servants of God should characterize an informed believer.

Satan

In the narrative of the temptation and the fall of man in Genesis 3, a wicked and malevolent seducer appears in the form of a serpent. Thus sin is introduced into the world, and death by sin. But where did this sin come from? We know that God created everything for His glory. He created some beings with free will. Both angels and humans can choose to do what is right or what is wrong. Some of these free beings abuse their privileges and disobey their Creator. This is proven by the existence of creatures such as Satan, fallen angels, and sinful human beings. We can be sure that God did not create them that way. When Jesus called Satan "a murderer from the beginning" (John 8:44), He meant the beginning of Satan's rebellion against God, not from the time God first created Satan.

Two passages in the prophets are generally believed to refer to the original fall of Satan. Isaiah 14:12-20 is directed first of all against the king of Babylon (v. 4); Ezekiel 28:11-19 is spoken to the king of Tyre. But in Ezekiel 28:2 the Spirit through Ezekiel addresses the prince of Tyre as if the words in verses 11-19 are for the power behind the throne—that is, Satan himself.

No doubt the enemies of Israel (Babylon and Tyre) were controlled by Satan. In these two poetic and prophetic passages the inspired eyes of God's servants see behind the veil of human government. The kings of Babylon and Tyre are seen as clear "types" of Satan. Many details could not apply to any mere man. (The same principle applies to other passages, especially in Psalms, which on the surface refer to a godly man but on closer study evidently are speaking of Christ Himself.) On this basis of interpretation, we learn several things about Satan: He was called **Lucifer**

("Light-bearer"), which translates a word meaning "The Morning Star" (Isaiah 14:12; by contrast, the true Morning Star is the Lord Jesus Christ, Revelation 22:16). He had a high position of trust and was both beautiful and wise (Ezek. 28:12-15). Lucifer was given charge of part of the universe. Sin entered God's creation for the first time when pride filled Lucifer's heart. He said, "I will ascend . . . I will exalt . . . I will sit . . . I will be like the Most High," like God Himself (Isa. 14:13-14).

Many angels, perhaps a third of them (Rev. 12:4), sided with Satan, shared in his sin, and fell with him: They were instantly cast from the immediate presence of God. Their final judgment is still future but absolutely certain (Isa. 14:12-15; Rev. 12:4, 9).

The Bible tells us much about Satan. His work, character, and personality may be learned by noting his various names in Scripture.

He is called the **wicked one** and as such snatches away the good seed of the gospel (Matt. 13:19) and sows tares (Matt. 13:28, 39). He hurls fiery darts of temptation to sin at believers, but these can be thwarted by faith (Eph. 6:16). Even new converts can overcome him and keep themselves so that he cannot touch them (1 John 2:13; 5:18). The Bible portrays the Wicked One as being opposed to God in every way.

> The Bible portrays the Wicked One as being opposed to God in every way.

He is called **the serpent**. Genesis 3:1-3 records how the serpent lied to Eve. In Genesis 4, Cain, who was "of that wicked one" (1 John 3:12) murdered his brother. Christ said the devil is "a **murderer** from the beginning and **the father of lies**" (John 8:44). In the serpent we see subtlety and venomous hate. Somewhat similar, though more violent in meaning, is the term **dragon** (Rev. 12:3, 7; 20:2).

He is called **Satan**. This is a Hebrew word meaning "adversary," as in Zechariah 3:1 (margin). Satan is always opposed to God and His people. Sometimes this opposition is open; he is described in 1 Peter 5:8 as a roaring lion whose goal it is to destroy a Christian's faith and testimony. Sometimes he disguises himself as an angel of light (2 Cor. 11:14). Satan's consistent purpose throughout his history, as revealed in the Bible, appears to be to oppose God in His purpose for the universe, especially regarding man.

One of his chief names is **the devil**, from the Greek for "accuser." It is used of Satan in four different ways:

1. He accuses men to God, as when he said that Job did not serve God for nothing (Job 1:9). He accuses the brethren before God day and night (Rev. 12:10).

2. He accuses God before the angels of heaven (Job 1:9) by casting aspersions on God's character (in this case, saying that God showed favoritism to Job). That this is an attack on the righteous government of God may be seen by considering the background. God had cast Satan and many other angels out of heaven because of the sin of rebellion. Satan implies that this is unrighteous and that God is unfair because He does not judge *man's* sins *at once.* One of the great purposes of the creation and redemption of man is that God may put to silence forever Satan's false accusations of unrighteousness.

3. The devil also accuses God to man (Gen. 3:5). He wants us to doubt God's love. Men criticize God for allowing people to suffer and for many other things. In this they are sharing in the work of the devil.

4. He accuses us to each other. For instance, he knew he would gain an advantage over Paul and the Corinthians if he could bring in some disagreement or misunderstanding (2 Cor. 2:11). Paul was not ignorant of his methods. Division among the Lord's people has greatly hindered the outreach of the gospel.

He is called **the tempter.** Satan succeeded only too well in tempting Adam and Eve. As we see in Genesis 3:6, he appealed to the lust of the flesh ("good for food"), the lust of the eyes ("pleasant to the eyes"), and the pride of life ("desirable to make one wise"). These three things are definitely "not of the Father" (1 John 2:16). Adam and Eve failed the test and fell into sin. Thousands of years later the tempter tried these same tactics on the last Adam, the Lord Jesus Christ. He said to Jesus, "Command this stone to become bread" (lust of the flesh). He followed this with "All this authority I will give You, and their glory" (lust of the eyes). Finally, he said, "If You are the Son of God, throw Yourself down from here" (pride of life). The tempter's greatest effort resulted in his greatest failure. Christ would not and could not sin. The complete story is recorded in Luke 4:1-13. See also Matthew 4:1-11 and Mark 1:12-13.

A number of other names of Satan may be grouped together: **Beelzebub, the ruler of the demons** (Matt. 12:24); the **prince of the power of the air** (Eph. 2:2; 6:12); **the ruler of this world** (John 12:31; 14:30; 16:11); and **the god of this world** (2 Cor. 4:4). These descriptions suggest Satan's greatest activity among men, ruling and deceiving this world, especially through the establishment and promotion of false religion. Every false religion in the world, as well as every cult and error in Christendom, may be considered a part of Satan's concentrated effort to substitute something other than Christ as the object of love and devotion of man's heart.

Satan is a personal, powerful being with cunning intelligence, personal feelings, and a will of his own. The idea that the devil is merely a personification of evil is wholly untenable in light of biblical revelation. Indeed, one of the best proofs of his personal activity in this modern world is that he has hoodwinked the masses into disbelieving in his existence, caricaturing him to make him merely a joking matter, and thus ridiculing those who accept the Bible's testimony.

The Fallen Angels

A Bible teaching that is even more widely disbelieved than the existence of Satan is the existence of demons or evil spirits—that is, fallen angels loose on earth. When we remember that the devil is not omniscient, omnipotent, or omnipresent, and that even God, who is all three of these, uses His angels to carry on His work, it should not surprise us that Satan uses his fallen followers to gain his desired ends.

> Whoever denies the reality of evil spirits denies the credibility of the gospel accounts and Christ's teachings.

Some of those who fell with Satan are already bound in chains, awaiting their judgment (2 Pet. 2:4; Jude 6). Others, however, are free to serve Satan's cause, possess human beings, cause sickness (though not all sickness is caused by them by any means), and otherwise torment men. The demons, or unclean spirits, were especially active during Christ's earthly ministry. Whoever denies the reality of these evil spirits denies the credibility of the gospel accounts and Christ's teachings. Mark chapter 5 is a classic passage on demon possession. The fact that demons may cause mental derangement, desire to inhabit bodies of people and even animals, and have rational and personal characteristics is made clear here. Demons may possess superhuman power and give it to evil men (Deut. 13:1-3; Matt. 24:24; Rev. 13:13-15). The gods of the heathen world, that is, the evil spirits that work behind the idols, were and are demons in many cases (1 Cor. 10:20).

Christ cast out demons and gave His disciples power to cast them out (Matt. 4:24; 10:1; Acts 19:12). There is never any hint that these demons were unreal or were merely psychological fixations of those possessed. Actual conversations are recorded between Christ and the demons. Missionaries in certain parts of the world have reported well-authenticated cases of demon-possession today. Western nations are not free from this destructive influence either.

There is no redemption for fallen angels, as there is for fallen man. It is likely that the angels knew what chances they were taking when they followed Lucifer; they therefore sinned in the face of greater light and privilege.

The devil himself will be cast out of heaven—from access to God's presence to accuse the brethren—and will wreak havoc on earth during the great tribulation, especially against Israel (Rev. 12:13-17). During the millennium, Satan will be bound in the Abyss (Rev. 20:1-3). After the millennium he will lead a brief but frantic rebellion against the King's government and His people (Rev. 20:7-9), and will finally be thrown into the lake of fire and brimstone (v. 10). Here he will be tormented "day and night forever and ever."

The angels that rebelled against a holy and righteous God along with the proud Lucifer will be judged and cast into the lake of fire that was prepared for the devil and his angels. There, along with all who rejected Christ and were followers of Satan (whether decent, religious, or immoral followers), they will suffer eternal punishment for their dreadful sin and guilt (Matt. 25:41). It is a solemn and frightful future that no human being needs to face if he will only put his trust in Christ alone as his Redeemer. Truly, we should be thankful that God provided redemption for fallen man through His Son!

2

ANTHROPOLOGY: THE STUDY OF MAN

Anthropology as a doctrine of Scripture has little connection with the branch of science by the same name. We are here concerned with the second great order of moral beings created by God—the human race. What does the Bible teach about man in God's plan?

The Origin of Man

Man would not be able to know the facts of his origin unless God told him about them. If God has given us a revelation of any kind, we may expect Him to tell us something of where we came from. God has revealed the essential facts in Genesis 1:27, 2:7, and other passages.

God formed the human body out of the dust of the ground. The human body is composed of common elements such as oxygen, hydrogen, carbon, and nitrogen. It is similar to the bodies of animals in many respects since it is made to live, breathe, and eat in the same environment. We read in Genesis 2:7 that God breathed into man the breath of life and he became a living soul. We also read that God created man in His own image (Gen. 1:26-27). This proves man's relation to God. God is Spirit (John 4:24), and man was created body, soul, and spirit in the image of God.

Despite its ongoing and deeply entrenching popularity, the theory of evolution does not explain the origin of matter of life. It also has tremendous gaps in its hypotheses regarding the origin of plant life, the origin of animal life, and the origin of human life. There are vast differences between the mineral, vegetable, animal, and human levels. It would seem that a desire to eliminate God leads evolutionists to overlook these difficulties.

The Bible teaches that Adam was the first man. He was a special creation of God. In God's time, by His own power, man became a "living soul" (Gen. 2:7). We recognize there are differing views about origins among true believers; for a more detailed discussion on the topic, consult the ECS course *Ready to Give an Answer.*

The Nature of Man

All Christians are agreed that man is more than a physical or material being. Man also has an immaterial part or parts to his make-up. Those who stress this twofold division of material and immaterial parts are called *dichotomists,* from two words meaning "to cut in two." To the dichotomists the soul, spirit, conscience, heart, etc., are all parts of the immaterial man, different from one another but alike in being facets of man's immaterial nature. Others, called *trichotomists,* believe that man is essentially tripartite (threefold), composed of body, soul, and spirit (1 Thess. 5:23; Heb. 4:12). The other characteristics, such as heart and conscience, are then viewed as functions (or facets) of the soul and spirit. Trichotomy is simpler and will be presented here, but with the admission that it is difficult to fit all of the terms into these three categories of body, soul, and spirit. Also, if a complete induction is made of the important words "heart," "conscience," and others, and even of "soul" and "spirit," there are overlappings. It should be stressed that both dichotomists and trichotomists may be orthodox believers and that the differences between these two views, when thoroughly examined, are comparatively minor.

The material part of man, **the body,** is subject to scientific investigation. Flesh, blood, bones, etc., compose this wonderful machine created originally by God. Due to the fall, the human body is a "lowly body" (Phil. 3:21). It is subject to disease, decay, and death. When Christ comes, the saints will receive new bodies like His (1 Cor. 15:53; 1 John 3:2). The death and resurrection of Christ guarantee the resurrection of all people. Sad to say, the wicked will rise from the dead only to face judgment for their sins (John 5:28-29).

The soul is the subject of self-conscious personal life (Ps. 13:2; 42:5, 11). While it can be directed toward heavenly things (Ps. 42:1-2), it can also be directed toward earthly and emotional things and is often closely associated with bodily appetites (compare Deuteronomy 12:15, 20; Psalms 107:9;

Proverbs 6:30; Isaiah 29:8). It displays a variety of emotional responses, such as desire (Deut. 12:20), hate (2 Sam. 5:8), vexation (2 Kings 4:27), rejoicing (Isa. 61:10), suffering (Gen. 42:21), and sorrow (Mark 14:34).

The principle of rational, ethical, and spiritual life is called **the spirit**. It is related to God in the saved person, but it is wrong to say that an unsaved person has no spirit (James 2:26 would make all unsaved people physically dead if that were so!). Animals have "souls" in the sense of emotional responses, and so forth, but they have no spirits with which to commune with God. The spirit is definitely different from the soul, but is not to be divided from it. Hebrews 4:12 points out that the Word can pierce through body ("joints and marrow"), soul, and spirit.

It should be noticed again that man, like God and the angels, has intellect, sensibility, and will, since he is a personal being.

—— ✑ ——

Man, like God and the angels, has intellect, sensibility, and will, since he is a personal being.

—— ✑ ——

The Origin and Propagation of the Immaterial Part of Man

Everyone knows that as to his physical being, a man is the product of procreation of his mother and father, as were his parents of their parents, and so forth back to Adam, the first man (though many today deny the historicity of Adam and Eve). There is no problem here in the physical realm, as science has carefully studied the process of conception and gestation. However, science can tell us nothing about the origin of our non-physical natures. (Some people, to escape this fact, have denied a separate existence to man's immaterial parts, making them only functions of physical organs, such as the brain. This is wholly inadequate and unscriptural.) Where, then, does the individual get his immaterial parts? There is controversy on this topic; we will only take time here to describe the one we believe best fits with Scripture—that is, traducianism.

Traducianism (the term simply means "to pass on") teaches that God created the entire man—material and immaterial—once for all in Adam and Eve, and that the entire nature is passed on from generation to generation. It is evident that God made Eve entirely out of Adam; there is no evidence that He created a soul for her. Also, He is said to have rested from creating after making man (Gen. 2:1-3). He would be continuously creating if there were no means of transmitting the immaterial parts of man through procreation. Traducianism accounts the best for our being "in Adam" and in ruin *by nature* (Rom. 5:12; 1 Cor. 15:22). It also explains the concept that individuals are in the "loins" of their ancestors (Gen. 46:26; Heb. 7:9-10). Of course, Christ partook of the complete nature of man and escaped sin. In accord with the virgin birth and Luke 1:35, it is clear that Christ was sanctified (set apart) from all of sin's condemnation and corruption from the instant of His miraculous conception by the Holy Spirit in Mary's virgin womb. Christ is an exception to so many things that it should not cause much trouble to see this.

The Position of Man

Psalm 8 reveals that man was created lower than the angels (v. 5) but higher than the animals (vv. 6-8). While God has no favorites (Acts 10:34), differences in rank exist among humans to facilitate ordered society. Scriptures like 1 Peter 2:13-14, Romans 13:1, and Ephesians 6:1 make it clear we are to submit to the authorities in our lives. Scripture also states that "the head of every man is Christ [and] the head of the woman is man" (1 Cor. 11:3). The reason for this position is that woman was second in creation and first in the fall. The Lord Jesus Christ is the Head of all creation (Heb. 2:6-9). See also Revelation 3:14, where the word "Beginning" means chief. Christ Himself is to deliver all to the Father in ages to come (1 Cor. 15:28).

The Free Will of Man

Within certain limits, God has given man free will. God made man in His own image. Man is a *person*; he is conscious of his own existence and his own responsibility to make the right choice. Of course, man is limited in the physical world; he cannot fly or run beyond a certain speed limit. And free will does not mean that man is at liberty to follow his own selfish desires without restraint. In a democracy, for instance, a man is "free," but he is expected to keep the laws of the land and respect the freedom of others.

In divine things, man is free to choose right or wrong, to do good or to do evil. In the garden of Eden, God gave man freedom with one minor restriction. Adam should have obeyed God. Adam was not under any compulsion from God to sin or not to sin. His "free will" made him responsible to do what was right. By choosing the wrong, Adam acquired a sinful nature, a tendency to sin. This sinful nature has been passed on to all his descendants, as is all too evident from the present state of society.

Function of Man

Why did God create man? The Westminster Shorter Catechism says, "The chief end of man is to glorify God and to enjoy Him forever." Out of God's own nature of love He created man so that He could love him and be loved by him. A creature without free will would have to obey God's commands mechanically. Love is only possible on the part of one who can withhold that love if he wishes to do so. The Father seeks people who are willing and desire to worship Him in spirit and in truth (John 4:23-24).

Another reason for man's creation is seen in relation to Satan. Satan led man into sin with the purpose of upsetting God's plans. Satan may well have assumed that man would only hate God for punishing him for his sin. This is all too often true. On the other hand, sin provided still more scope for God to show His love. "Where sin abounded, grace abounded much more" (Rom. 5:20). Because of the cross of Christ, Satan's accusations will be silenced forever. Christ will have a vast host of the redeemed with Him throughout eternity.

The Responsibility of Man

God's greatest overall plan is to glorify His Son, the Lord Jesus Christ. Man was created for a special place in this program. Man is responsible to learn God's will and to do it. He should use his free will for God's glory, to help establish God's purposes to honor the Son (1 Cor. 10:31; Col. 1:18).

> *Man should use his free will for God's glory, to help establish God's purposes to honor the Son.*

Man has inherited a sinful nature from Adam, but in Christ he may have the capability of choosing the right and rejecting the wrong. The term *total depravity* means that natural man is unable to please God. Far from excusing man's sin, the Bible teaches our inability to earn salvation and our desperate need of a Savior. Depravity does not mean that each man is as bad as he can be or that he can do no "good" thing to his fellow man. We know this is not true. But what is "good" to men is not up to God's standards. Civic decency will win human respect but will never get us to heaven.

3

HAMARTIOLOGY: THE STUDY OF SIN

Hamartiology (from the Greek word *hamartia*, meaning "sin") is the study of sin. In this section we will examine the definition of sin, its origin on earth, and differences between personal sin, the inherited sin nature, and imputed sin.

Defining Sin

Many words in the Bible refer to sin: eight main ones in the Old Testament and twelve in the New. Some of the ideas conveyed by these words are: missing the right mark and hitting the wrong one; transgression (passing over a prescribed line); perversion; disobedience; rebellion; a misstep; a debt; ignorance of what should be known; lawlessness; and diminishing what should be given in full.

> Sin can be defined as any lack of conformity to God's character, especially as it is expressed for us in the Word.

Human concepts of sin as mere finiteness, illusion, sensuality, ignorance, or selfishness are inadequate. Generally speaking, sin can be defined as *any lack of conformity to God's character, especially as it is expressed for us in the Word*. We should not water down the definition to include only the willful practice of certain things, since lack of conformity to God and His will involve both pollution and guilt.

The Origin of Sin

God created beings that could love Him and serve Him freely. This is the same as saying that He created beings that could do the opposite, that are capable of sinning, for if they could not disobey, they would have to obey under compulsion. If they could choose to sin or to obey, some would be free to choose to sin. Some did sin. The first one, as we have seen, was Lucifer (Isa. 14; Ezek. 28).

The story of Adam's fall into sin in Genesis 3 is well known, but the following points are important. In the garden of Eden all circumstances were favorable to Adam. He could eat the fruit of trees already planted. He was the head of the submissive animal world. (By contrast, Christ, "the last Adam," was tempted in the wilderness after forty days with wild animals for company and not sustained by any food.) Adam had daily conversation with God. There was only one restriction: he was not to eat any fruit of the tree of the knowledge of good and evil. Satan made the first approach by going, not to Adam, but to Eve. He planted a doubt in her mind by raising a question about the goodness of God. God had said not to eat any of its fruit. If they did they would die. Satan said they would *not* die. He promised they would be like God and know good and evil. Eve was deceived and believed this. Adam's sin was worse because he was not deceived. He understood to some extent what he was doing (1 Tim. 2:14).

Was Satan's promise fulfilled? After they had sinned, they did know evil by experience. There was some truth in what Satan said. Even God knows in His mind the difference between good and evil, but He does not know evil experientially. Everything He does is good. Adam was plainly warned. God had said that in the very day he disobeyed he would die (Gen. 2:17) and separation from God set in immediately, along with guilt and shame. Furthermore, Adam and Eve began to die physically from that moment as sin had its effect on their physical make-up. "The wages of sin is death."

Personal Sin

Adam's sin was personal, and because of it all human beings inherit a sin nature and have his sin imputed to them. For us today the order is the opposite. We have the inherited sin nature and as a result we sin personally. We are not sinners merely because we sin (though this is also true); we sin because we are sinners. Many people mistakenly believe that if they could just stop their personal sinning, they would be fit for heaven. However, past sins need to be taken care of—and not only is it impossible to be sinlessly perfect now (1 John 1:8), but the sin *nature* needs to be accounted for. We *are* much worse than we *act!* The number and variety of personal sins is almost endless. Some lists of them may be found in Mark 7:21, 22; Romans 1:29-31; Galatians 5:19-21. Personal sins bring condemnation and guilt in the eyes of God.

God's remedy is twofold, negative and positive. In the negative sense, forgiveness is the remedy, which is a releasing—a sending away—a pardoning of sins, through the blood of Christ. Judicial guilt and condemnation are done away with. Forgiveness comes through confession— that is, agreeing to God's diagnosis of our sinful condition. In the positive sense, God's remedy for personal sin is justification—a legal declaration that the believer in Christ is just (righteous) because he actually *is* so through the righteousness of Christ which is imputed to him ("reckoned" to his "account"—see Romans 3:22 and 2 Corinthians 5:21). The basis for God's forgiving and justifying us is the sacrificial, substitutionary death of Christ at Calvary.

The Inherited Sin Nature

An illustration from nature helps here: The inherited sin nature may be compared to the root of a tree of which individual personal sins are the fruits. The sin nature is the terrible effect on the body, the soul, and the spirit as a result of being separated from God. It is a fallen state that produces sin and

> Having inherited this nature to sin, it is impossible to please God in our natural condition.

disease. Having inherited this state—this nature to sin—it is impossible to please God in our natural condition, and it cannot be eradicated or even refined in this life.

This sin nature is the only nature unsaved people possess. Christians possess this old nature plus a new, divine nature (2 Pet. 1:4)—hence the inner conflict. The former is incapable of good before God (Rom. 7:18) and the latter is incapable of sin (1 John 3:9). The inherited sin nature brings condemnation. Corruption, depravity, and blindness and darkness in spiritual things are all results of inherited sin. The heart of man is "desperately wicked" (Jer. 17:9), and only a completely new birth can qualify man for God's kingdom (John 3:6). In stressing the depravity of man, it should again be pointed out that the Bible does not teach that men have no appreciation or enjoyment of good, that they have no conscience, or that they actually carry out all their lusts. The penalty for the sin nature is separation from God, and unless this is remedied through faith in Christ, it will be a fixed "second death" through all eternity.

—————— ஒ ——————

The heart of man is desperately wicked, and only a completely new birth can qualify man for God's kingdom.

—————— ஒ ——————

The remedy is twofold: God judges the sin nature in the light of the cross (Rom. 8:1; Gal. 2:20; 5:24) and the gift of the Holy Spirit makes victory over this judged sin nature possible (chapters 6 and 8 of Romans; Galatians 5:16). Finally, at death or the rapture the believer's sin nature will be completely eradicated.

Imputed Sin

To *impute* is to reckon something to a person, to ascribe responsibility to a person as the originator, and to count as belonging to another. A good biblical example is in Philemon 18, where Paul asks that any debt the runaway slave Onesimus had incurred be charged to his account. This was judicial imputation, since it was not Paul's debt to begin with. The imputation of Adam's sin to all of us humans is real because it was ours to begin with, since we acted in Adam (Rom. 5:12; Gal. 3:22). As we have seen before, one of the arguments for traducianism (compare Hebrews 7:9-10) is that the whole person was in the ancestor and acting in him. In Romans 5:12, the word "sinned" is a good translation because it was one act done by the whole race in Adam. In like manner, Christ's righteousness is imputed to all believers. Romans 5:14 shows that the penalty for this imputed sin is physical death ("death reigned"). In Adam all die and in Christ all are made alive—or more definitively, all who are in Christ are made alive. The NASB translates Romans 3:23 "all sinned" rather than "all have sinned," meaning that we all sinned in Adam at a point in time (same thought as in Romans 5:12). The continual "falling short" refers to personal sins growing out of this imputed sin of Adam.

The joint action with Adam was impersonal and unconscious on our part, but it incurred guilt and condemnation to physical death. God's remedy for imputed sin is imputed righteousness. First our sin was imputed to Christ on the cross (2 Cor. 5:21; 1 Pet. 2:24; Isa. 53:6). Then the individual believer has the righteousness of God procured by Christ on the cross imputed to him (2 Cor. 5:21b; 1 Cor. 1:30). Believers are no longer guilty, condemned sinners, but are guaranteed life forever. Could anything be more wonderful than God's remedy for sin?

The Christian's Sin and Its Remedy

Every well-taught Christian knows that he sins, and even those who are taught otherwise must realize in their more honest moments that they fall short of God's glory. First John 1:8-10 makes it clear that we do sin, and this causes conflict with the indwelling Holy Spirit (Gal. 5:17). Since Christ is the Christian's standard and our light is greater than anyone else's, and since we are in God's family, it is possible that a believer's sin is worse than that of an unsaved person. The Christian has three notorious enemies in this life, each one luring him into sin if possible.

The world is the ordered system of this Satan-dominated age—the world of Christ-rejecting unbelievers (John 15:18-19). It does not refer to God's creation ("nature"). First John 5:4-5 gives the secret of victory over the world as our new nature born of God, which is inclined toward His commands (5:4a), our faith, which is identified with Christ's victory when we first believed (5:4b) and our character of believing in the Son in defiance of the world's unbelief (5:5).

> Victory over the flesh comes from constantly ordering our daily lives in dependence on the Holy Spirit.

The flesh refers not only to sensual sins, but also to the remains of the sin nature which linger after regeneration, including the ethical and spiritual constitution that is in conflict with the Spirit. Victory over the flesh comes from constantly ordering our daily lives in dependence on the Holy Spirit (Gal. 5:16) to overcome the natural characteristic of the flesh to be independent of God.

The devil is our third foe. Satan's strategy is methodical and clever (Eph. 6:11); we are in a virtual ongoing wrestling match with him (6:12). The secret of victory over the devil is to resist him when he advances in a friendly manner (James 4:7b) or when he attacks fiercely (1 Pet. 5:8-9) and to rely on divine provision solely—the Spirit (1 John 4:4), submission to God (James 4:7), faith (1 Pet. 5:9), and the whole armor of God that has been provided to us (Eph. 6:11-17).

Finally, sin may be prevented by treasuring up the Word of God in our hearts (Ps. 119:11) and by allowing the Spirit to lead us to truth (John 16:13ff) and service (Rom. 8:14). Christ does exercise His High-priestly ministry on our behalf (Heb. 7:25), but we must use God's Word as a preventive to sin and to cooperate with the Holy Spirit's ministry in us.

> *We should be thankful to God's discipline that brings us back to Him before we ruin our testimony.*

If we go on in sin without confessing it (1 John 1:9), then we can expect chastisement and even death. Sin in the believer's life brings darkness and kills joy, fellowship, and confidence in prayer. It will also cause shame at the rapture. We should be thankful for God's discipline that brings us back to Him before we ruin our testimony. Confession is the key word for sinning Christians, and since sin is a dreadful thing in God's holy eyes, it is wise to keep very short accounts with God and not wait till sins accumulate before we confess them. The closer a person lives to our holy God, the more sinful he will seem to himself. It is one of the paradoxes of Christianity that the godliest and sweetest of Christ's saints have always felt themselves to be the deepest-dyed sinners.

4

SOTERIOLOGY: THE STUDY OF SALVATION – PART 1 –

The study of sin showed us clearly the great need for salvation. The study of salvation is called Soteriology, from the Greek word for "savior" (*soter*).

The Finished Work of Christ

When Christ died on the cross, He cried out in triumph "It is finished!" (John 19:30). The finished work of Christ does not guarantee that everyone is already saved, but it does mean that He has made provision for all people to *be* saved. Four words sum up the chief aspects of the finished work of Christ.

There is **substitution**. The law of God says, "The soul who sins shall die" (Ezek. 18:20). God could not set aside His own laws, yet love had to find a way to satisfy the just claims of His holiness. There had to be a substitute, one who would die for the guilty. If not, the guilty man would have to die for his own sins, and there would be no salvation. This substitute had to be

- ➤ *Acceptable to God.* Some other plan might seem reasonable to man, but God is the Judge and He must be satisfied.
- ➤ *Equal to the condemned person.* Animals are inferior (Heb. 10:4). Angels are superior to men, but they are spirits, without bodies, and so cannot die. The suitable substitute had to have a corporeal body.

> *Innocent.* No man with even one sin of his own could act as a substitute for another. Such a man would have to die for his own sin.

> *Willing to die.* It would not be righteous for God to compel some innocent person to die for another. The devil would soon have brought this accusation against God.

> *Possessed of an infinite life.* The death of a mere man, even if innocent, would be sufficient for only one other man. God's law is "life shall be for life" (Deut. 19:21). Only Deity is infinite. In other words, the Perfect Substitute had to be God Himself.

Obviously no one could fulfill these requirements except the God-Man, the Lord Jesus Christ. As God, He is co-equal with the Father and the Spirit. As man, He was sinless. The life of the God-Man, willingly laid down, was an infinite life, and the praise and adoration of saved creatures goes to God Himself.

Although the word "substitute" is hardly to be found in any version of the Bible, the idea of vicarious or substitutionary suffering may be found throughout. Animal sacrifices in the Old Testament were accepted by God as pictures of a coming Christ. For instance, God accepted Abel's lamb but rejected Cain's bloodless offering (Gen. 4:4-5). God Himself provided a ram to die in the place of Isaac (Gen. 22:13). Under the Levitical system, the people of Israel throughout their history offered literally millions of animals in sacrifice to God. The truth of substitution is evident in Isaiah 53 (see vv. 5, 8, 10, 12).

In the New Testament, Jesus spoke of His body given for us and of His blood shed for us (Luke 22:19-20). Paul and Peter taught the truth of substitution over and over (e.g., Rom. 5:8; Gal. 3:13; 1 Pet. 3:18). We see, then, that

> **Christ died for sinners and He also died for sins.**

Christ died for sinners—that is, in their place, on their behalf, or for their benefit. He also died for sins, Himself taking on the responsibility for the penalty. Christ the Son of God, the perfect man, is the ideal, adequate, and only Substitute!

There is **redemption**. The word *redeem* means "to buy" or "to buy back again." Redemption has to do with sin and release from its bondage. An Old

Testament illustration is seen in the case of the man who through sickness or poverty might have to sell his property. According to the Mosaic law, his relative, called a *goel,* or kinsman-redeemer, had the legal right to buy it back at any time. In this way they would keep the property in the family (Lev. 25:23-25). See also Ruth 4:1-10 and Jeremiah 32:6-12.

There are five Greek verbs translated "redeem," "purchase," etc., in the New Testament. These words show a divine progression and teach that, while the work of Christ is an adequate provision for all people, it is effective only to those who believe.

> **While the work of Christ is an adequate provision for all people, it is effective only to those who believe.**

The first word means "to frequent a market" or "to buy in a market" (Matt. 13:45, 46; Luke 9:13). Everyone, including the worst possible sinner, is ransomed or bought in a provisional sense (2 Pet. 2:1). The believer's body is bought with a price (1 Cor. 6:20). We are purchased by blood to be a kingdom and priests (Rev. 5:9-10). The second word is like the first, but the addition of a prefix (*ex*) that means that the purchase is removed from sale and the process cannot be reversed. This word can be used only of believers, those who accept Christ's provision (Gal. 3:13; 4:5).

The third word suggests release upon receipt of payment. First Peter 1:18-19 indicates that the price is the precious blood of Christ, and Titus 2:14 shows that we are redeemed from iniquity for His possession. The fourth word is like the third, with the addition of a prefix (*apo*) that strengthens the idea of release "away from," and occurs in the noun form in Romans 3:24 and Ephesians 1:14.

The fifth word has a somewhat different root meaning from the preceding words but is translated "purchase" in Acts 20:28. The idea is that God has taken for Himself and kept the church which He "purchased with His own blood." By nature, man belongs to God because God created him. But through sin man came under the control of another. Christ paid the ransom; in fact, He gave all He had—Himself—to buy "the pearl of great price" (the church He loves).

These words we have looked at are instructive, but the metaphors should not be pressed beyond scriptural warrant. For example, it does not say to whom the ransom was paid—it certainly was not to Satan! In view of the great doctrine of redemption by blood, it is no wonder that Christian hymnals are full of great hymns to the Redeemer and the glory of being among the redeemed!

There is **propitiation**. Not only has Christ completed the work of redeeming us from sin, but He has satisfied God, or "propitiated" Him. Propitiation is the value of Christ's death to satisfy God and let Him act in love toward sinners without violating His righteousness, holiness, or justice. The idea that the Father is wrathful and the gentle Jesus appeased Him is unworthy of consideration. Actually, 1 John 4:10 shows love as the motive for God sending His Son as the propitiation for our sins. First John 2:2 shows that the satisfaction is all-inclusive: "Not for our's only but also for the whole world." Wrath results when God is not propitiated. The same word is used in the New Testament to translate the Old Testament word for "mercy seat" into Greek (Heb. 9:5) and for propitiation (Romans 3:25, speaking of Christ). The mercy seat spoke of covering of sin and the divine standard of righteousness that demanded it.

———— ❧ ————

Propitiation enables God to freely and justly forgive all sin, impute all righteousness, and bestow all grace and glory on sinners.

———— ❧ ————

Luke 18:13, the publican's prayer, is best translated, "God, be propitiated to me a sinner." God is satisfied with Christ's work in paying the penalty for sin. It was a once-for-all act (Heb. 9:28). Propitiation enables God to freely and justly forgive all sin, impute all righteousness, and bestow all grace and glory on sinners. It is unnecessary to beg God to be "merciful," as He already is such. Believe that He is propitious and is perfectly satisfied with Jesus and His work. He is. We should be too.

There is **reconciliation**. Substitution, redemption toward sin, propitiation of God, and now reconciliation of man—these are the chief accomplishments of the sufferings and death of Christ. We have seen under hamartiology that His death provided for the judgment of the sin nature and is the basis for forgiveness and cleansing, two other great accomplishments.

It is a common error to say that God was reconciled to man. The Bible actually teaches that *man* is the one who is to be reconciled. In common usage, reconciliation is understood as a bringing together of parties that were at odds with each other. Reconciliation means a complete change of position. Reconciliation changes the position of enmity to one of amity or friendship, and this is through the blood (sacrificial death) of Christ (Col. 1:20) and because of Christ's death, there is both a provisional and an actual aspect to reconciliation.

Provisionally, the whole world is reconciled to God (2 Cor. 5:14-15, 19). This means that the world can be saved now. It does not mean that the whole world is or will be saved; it means that the whole world is savable. The actual reconciliation is commanded in 2 Corinthians 5:20: "Be reconciled to God," (which, in its context, is Paul's summary of his message to sinners, not an appeal to the Corinthians, who were already reconciled to God). All things become new when a person is reconciled, and his position is exchanged from "in Adam" to "in Christ" and from sin to righteousness. Sins are remitted, there is a new creation, and the believer is saved. It should also be noted that things in heaven are reconciled—that is, angelic thrones, principalities, and powers (Col. 1:16, 20).

Election

We are not called upon to understand all of God's ways, but we are called upon to accept what the Bible teaches, even if it does not appeal to the mind of man. The doctrine of **election** (meaning, "choosing" or "picking out") is one of the most difficult of all scriptural teachings. To say that God picks out those whom He knew ahead of

> God does not "send" anyone to the lake of fire; people go there because they have rejected Christ.

time would choose Him is not election by God—that would merely be God putting an endorsement on *man's* "election." It is true that man has freedom of the will and must believe in Christ to be saved. But it is also true that God chose some to be saved. No one deserved to be saved, and so God in grace chose some to give to Christ (John 6:37). Nowhere does it say, however, that anyone was elected to be lost. The lake of fire was prepared for the devil and his angels. God does not "send" anyone there; people go there because they have rejected Christ. Romans 9 is the classic passage on election, even though it is not about believers in the church. Angels, Israel, and even Christ are all spoken of as "elect" (1 Tim. 5:21; Isa. 45:3-4; 1 Pet. 2:6). Christians are called "elect" in Romans 8:33; Colossians 3:12; 1 Peter 1:2.

Since no one deserved salvation it is not unfair of God to choose some to be saved and pass over others. These others are responsible beings who reject the gospel of their own will. Election is an encouragement to the believer that everything that happens to him has a purpose in God's plan. Being chosen is an incentive to service. Most important of all, election exalts the sovereignty of God. A person who has difficulties with election should make a study with the help of a concordance of such words as "elect," "choose," and "predestine." Predestination has more to do with being made conformable to Christ than do election (Rom. 8:29) and adoption (Eph. 1:5, 11).

Associated with election is **calling**. "Whom he did predestine, these he also called" (Rom. 8:30). The means of calling is the gospel (2 Thess. 2:14). *Calling* is the act whereby God summons men to Himself in salvation. It has both a general and an effectual aspect.

The general call invites all people to come to God and is related to "drawing" all people to Christ (John 12:32). Many reject the general call and will be held responsible for this (Heb. 12:25). The effectual or efficacious call results in certain salvation. It is related to "drawing" in John 6:37, 44. Those whom the Father has given to His Son will definitely come to Christ and be accepted by Him. No one is compelled to accept the gospel; rather, the elect are made willing. Those so called of God are as good as glorified, so certain is the outcome of salvation (Rom. 8:39); the One who is calling will most certainly do it (1 Thess. 5:24).

While the outcome of the call is certain, the means is the gospel—hence, it must be preached. Those who have not heard the gospel will be judged by the light they have in nature, conscience, and remnants of primitive truth (which most cultures have preserved from ancient times even in the midst of gross error). The Judge of all the earth (as He is called in Genesis 18:25) will do right regarding these heathen people; undoubtedly, their responsibility is much less than that of those who reject Christ in a land where there are many gospel-preaching churches and Christian radio programs, literature, etc.

The Convicting Work of the Spirit

Apart from the work of the Holy Spirit no one would be saved. In their natural state, human beings are dead in sins (Eph. 2:1-3) and blinded by Satan (2 Cor. 4:3-4). The "natural" man does not accept the things of God's Spirit (1 Cor. 2:14) and not one of them is seeking God (Rom. 3:10-18). Pressures brought upon people apart from prayer and preaching of the gospel often result in professions of salvation which are devoid of reality.

The Holy Spirit today is convicting sinners throughout the world regarding sin, righteousness, and judgment (John 16:8). Those so convicted do not necessarily act upon the conviction, but they do recognize it. First of all, sinners are convicted of the one great sin of unbelief in Christ (John 16:9). Then they are convicted of righteousness because Christ is going to the Father (v. 10). This may mean that Christ's going to the Father proves His righteousness (even though He died a criminal's death on the accursed tree). He is the standard of righteousness as the glorified man. Or it may mean that without the very righteousness of a person will never follow Him into the presence of the Father in heaven. Christ's righteousness is imputed to the believer the moment he or she believes in Him. Thirdly, men are convicted of judgment (v. 11). This refers to the judgment of Satan at the cross. If the leader of sin was so judged, it is certain that his followers will also be judged for participating in his world system (whether they know they did Satan's work or not).

The practical lesson for us to learn is that the Holy Spirit does this convicting through the biblical message of the gospel of Christ, whether written or spoken.

The "Terms" of Salvation

"Believe on the Lord Jesus Christ, and you will be saved" (Acts 16:31). These are the "terms" of salvation. Men have been seeking to add all sorts of works and rites to this simple gospel for centuries—additions which can only cancel out the fact that salvation is strictly by grace through faith plus nothing (Eph. 2:8-9). Repentance is a part of belief, since one cannot truly believe or have faith without changing one's mind about the past. *Repent* simply means to change one's mind. Emotion may occur when one is converted, though not necessarily. The idea that one has to weep and "pray through" has no factual, biblical basis. Some people like to make oral confession, water baptism, the lordship of Christ, or other things a part of salvation. They are not. These are proper consequences of salvation, but *faith alone* is the channel through which God graciously gives us salvation—nothing else is required.

A typical secular definition of faith might be "the assent of the mind to what is declared by another." Spiritually saving faith, however, involves much more than simple mental assent or agreement. God has revealed His love and the Christian tells the gospel story. If the hearer believes the message in his heart as well as in his head, he has faith. Trust, confidence, and restful reliance on God are aspects of faith. Faith is the hand of the heart

——— ❧ ———

Faith alone is the channel through which God graciously gives us salvation—nothing else is required.

——— ❧ ———

that reaches out to accept the free gift of salvation. Only the Holy Spirit can give a person true faith. The purpose of this is that God may get the glory and that no man may have grounds for boasting. Faith comes from hearing (which includes reading) the word spoken or written about Christ—that is, the gospel (Rom. 10:17). Faith must be grounded in or based on God's own testimony about His Son that is recorded for us in the Bible (1 John 5:7-9).

——— ❧ ———

It is every Christian's privilege to proclaim the gospel, if not on a platform, certainly in daily life.

——— ❧ ———

In the New Testament, *faith* and *believe* are the same word in the Greek. Faith is a noun, believe is a verb—that is, it is faith in action that rests on—trusts—Jesus Christ. People sometimes speak of "coming to faith," but the Bible repeatedly makes it clear that saving faith must have the right focus or object. People can have faith in all sorts of things, ideas, or objects. *But God gives salvation only to those who believe in Jesus Christ.* It is faith in the Lord Jesus Christ that brings salvation.

When speaking or preaching the gospel, we should give the hearers something upon which they can rest their faith—namely, the good news of salvation by faith in Christ backed up with biblical references. The Holy Spirit does not convict through our own personalities so much as through the Word itself. It is every Christian's privilege to proclaim the gospel, if not on a platform, certainly in daily life.

5

SOTERIOLOGY: THE STUDY OF SALVATION – PART 2 –

The Saving Work of God

We have seen how Christ on the cross finished the work that God gave Him to do by providing Himself as a Substitute for us sinners and also redemption toward sin, propitiation of God, and reconciliation of man. We have seen how these provisions become effectual only for those who are convicted by the Holy Spirit and have put their faith in Jesus Christ. Now we must see how the Father does His saving work for sinners as they put their trust in His Son, thus completing the work of each Member of the Godhead in this great work of salvation.

Already we have studied enough Soteriology to know that salvation is much, much greater than a mere "fire-escape" from hell. But the saving work of God the Father will add even greater testimony to this fact. Dr. L. S. Chafer has listed and described thirty-three things that God does for the sinner the moment he believes! (See Volume III of Chafer's *Systematic Theology* under "The Riches of Divine Grace.") We shall mention just a few.

> **Salvation is much, much greater than a mere "fire escape" from hell.**

There is **justification**. Justification by faith is one of the most important doctrines of the Christian faith. Forgiveness is negative—removing something—whereas justification is positive—adding something to the believer. The ungodly are justified by God (Rom. 4:5). This means God declares them righteous because they are righteous in Christ when they believe. To justify is not to make righteous or to be righteous, but to declare righteous in a legal sense. ("Just" and "righteous" mean exactly the same thing.) Sinners who accept Christ are "justified freely by His grace" (Rom. 3:24). Justification is based on the redemption secured by Christ Jesus. While Galatians has a great deal in it about justification, the letter to the Romans is the classic book on this doctrine as to how (by what means) justification comes. It is by grace (3:24)—God's free favor to man; by faith (5:1)—man's acceptance of God's offer; by blood (5:9)—the price of Christ's death and it is by righteousness (5:18-19)—Christ's obedience on the cross. The results of the justification seen in Romans are peace (Isa. 32:17; Rom. 5:1), freedom from condemnation (Rom. 8:33-34), heirship (Titus 3:7; Rom. 8:17), and glorification (Rom. 8:30).

"Justification by works" as described in James 2:21, 25 is an altogether different kind of justification from that described above. It is justification in the sight of *men* and is achieved only by a godly, consistent Christian life. This is an important type of justification, but it can be acquired only after we have been justified in God's sight by faith in Christ apart from works.

There is **regeneration**. The separation of man from God is viewed in Scripture as "spiritual death." It is the result of sin (Eph. 2:1). Every person on earth is born with the same natural life which Adam had. This life is suitable for existence on this planet and under certain conditions in outer space, but it is not at all suitable for existence in heaven. "Unless one is born again, he cannot see the kingdom of God" (John 3:3).

——————— ❧ ———————

The separation of man from God is viewed in Scripture as "Spiritual death."

——————— ❧ ———————

We are born again by the Spirit of God and by the gospel message that has been preserved in God's written Word (John 3:5; 1 Pet. 1:22-25). We are not born children of God by blood (natural birth), by the will of the flesh (self determination or self effort), or by the will of man (the action of someone else, by priestly intercession or water baptism). Those who are born sons of God get this authority by receiving Christ, by believing in His name (John 1:12-13).

By regeneration we are born again, we receive new life, we become new creations in Christ Jesus. Old things are passed away, all things are new (2 Cor. 5:17). We put on the new man (Col. 3:10). We can and should walk in newness of life. As sons of God we are also heirs of God (Gal. 4:7) and co-heirs with Christ (Rom. 8:17). As sons we are also subject to the Father's chastening, which is only for sons, the ones He loves (Heb. 12:6).

In summary, then, regeneration, or rebirth, is the impartation of eternal life in the spiritual realm. Only the regenerated are saved from eternal damnation and only God can regenerate us. His purpose in regeneration is that we should be a kind of first-fruits of His creatures (James 1:18), heirs of an inheritance (1 Pet. 1:3-4), and doers of good works (Eph. 2:10).

There is **adoption**. This term occurs only in the Pauline Epistles. It is not to be confused with the modern concept of "adopting" children not born in the family at all. It is rather a declaration by God that He accepts His regenerated children as sons with all the legal rights of inheritance in Christ. Like all the other things in the saving work of God, it is received by faith at the moment of salvation, whether the believer knows about the doctrine or not (just as a newborn child receives all the benefits of being born into a fine family at the moment of physical birth without realizing it till later). It is not a so-called "second blessing." While we were made sons at regeneration, we will be manifested as such when Christ comes in glory. We already have the "Spirit of adoption," but we still await its full manifestation, i.e. "the redemption of our body" (Rom. 8:15, 23). The evidences of sonship in the Christian's life are: (1) being led by the Spirit (Rom. 8:14), separation from the world (2 Cor. 6:14-18), the overcoming life (Rev. 21:7), and chastening discipline of the Father (Heb. 12:6-8).

There is **sanctification**. There is a daily practical sanctification, and there is also the positional sanctification we receive at salvation. To *sanctify* means to set apart for some special purpose. The key idea is separation. In the past the believer is separated from the penalty of sin, in the present from the power of sin, and in the future from the presence of sin. The practical outworking of this is based upon the fact that every believer is a "saint" (from the same Greek word as "sanctify") of God from the moment he or she believes in Christ, and should therefore act accordingly. Men change the order and say those who live good lives may later be declared saints. Hebrews 10:10-14 shows that this positional sanctification was once for all and cannot be repeated. It is absolute, since Christ Himself is our Sanctification (1 Cor. 1:30). All believers have been set apart (sanctified) perfectly forever in Christ at the moment of salvation. Now it is the duty of each to become progressively more "holy" (separated from sin) through the Word of God (John 17:17; 1 Pet. 1:15-16).

———— ❧ ————
Because we have been forgiven, we should forgive one another.
———— ❧ ————

There is **forgiveness**. Justification is an acknowledgment of righteousness received from Christ; forgiveness is the release of sins, the subtraction of unrighteousness. It is easy to understand this doctrine because we see the human counterpart in our daily lives, "as we . . . forgive everyone who is indebted to us" (Luke 11:4). Positionally, forgiveness means that all past, present, and future sins were forgiven when we believed (Eph. 1:7; 4:32; Col. 1:14; 2:13). Practically, in order to be in fellowship with the Father, we should confess our sins to Him through Christ each time we fail (1 John 1:9). Some people have difficulty believing that our future sins could already be forgiven, forgetting that all our sins were future when Christ died. All our sins were taken away—remitted in full—when we believed, because Christ bore the penalty for them on the cross. Because we have been forgiven, we should forgive one another (Eph. 4:32). We should also forget, as God has (Heb. 8:12). The result of forgiveness of sins should be a great joy and peace.

There is **access to God**—the right of entry to God's presence. It is obtained by faith and opens to the unlimited blessings of God (Rom. 5:2). Believing Jews and Gentiles have access to the presence of the Father by the one Holy Spirit (Eph. 2:18). It is based on the reconciling work of Christ and is accompanied by perfect confidence (Eph. 3:12; Heb. 4:16; 10:19-20).

There is **freedom from the Law**. The Law was a restraint for the ungodly (1 Tim. 1:9), but never a way of salvation, not even during the Old Testament era. There are rules under grace (the New Testament is full of commands but not in a legalistic framework of punishment for disobedience) but Christians are not under law as a rule of

———— ❧ ————
Grace is a much higher statement of God's standard of living than the Law could ever be.
———— ❧ ————

life. We are *free* from the Law (Rom. 8:2); we are *dead* to the Law (Rom. 7:4) and we are *delivered* from the Law (Rom. 7:6). All this occurred at the moment of salvation along with the other parts of God's saving work. Christians respect the Mosaic law as one statement of God's standard of holiness, but grace is a much higher statement of God's standard of living than the Law could ever be.

Assurance and Security

> To know that one is saved now is assurance; to know that one is saved forever is security.

One of the most reassuring doctrines of the New Testament is that once a person has been saved he can never again be lost. To know that one is saved now is assurance; to know that one is saved forever is security. Many have the former but believe the latter is impossible or presumptuous. Unfortunately, some who call themselves Christians have neither. Most problems in this regard come from faulty teaching, natural fears, and a misunderstanding of what salvation really is.

Assurance

Study carefully 1 John 5:13; 1 John 3:1; John 3:36; and John 5:24. These are some of the well-known verses for assurance. There are many more. The Word of God is the primary source of assurance. The basis of our salvation is Christ's death, but the basis of our assurance is God's saying that it is so ("believes Him who sent Me"). God cannot lie or change His mind.

Two other important evidences of salvation are Christian experience and the inner witness of the Spirit. Experience does not mean our feelings (they change with the weather, health, circumstances, etc), but rather the deep consciousness of the things of God. If one's doctrine is wrong or one is living out of fellowship with God, of course the experience will not be very encouraging! Normal Christian experience includes love for other believers (1 John 3:14; Rom. 8:29), understanding and desire for the Bible (1 Cor. 2:14), conviction of sin (1 John 1:5-10; 3:7-14), good works (James 2:14-26), consciousness of the Fatherhood of God (Matt. 11:27) and of the indwelling Christ (2 Cor. 13:5) and a desire to see others share in the Christian faith. The internal ministry of the Spirit includes filling us with God's love (Rom. 5:5), guiding us (Rom. 8:14), and witnessing to us (Rom. 8:16).

The important thing is what we believe rather than the emotional experiences involved in our conversion, the style of preaching we heard, or our complete understanding of the gospel. Did we believe the gospel of salvation by grace through faith? Did we reach out the hand of faith to accept salvation as a free gift from the Lord? If so, we can have absolute assurance of salvation.

Eternal Security

Many who have assurance of salvation now and have the evidences of new life still ask that most important question—"Can a truly born again Christian ever be lost?" Many people say a "backslider" (a professing Christian whose life does not reflect that) can lose his salvation and go to hell. They say that if we could be sure of unconditional *eternal* life, we could live on in sin without fear of judgment. They forget that God's chastening, even to the point of death, would take care of this. Moreover, the unclean and lustful are simply false professors and enemies of the cross (Eph. 5:5-6; Phil. 3:18-19).

What do the Scriptures say about security? Read John 10:27, 28; 1 Peter 1:5; John 11:26; 2 Timothy 1:12; Hebrews 7:25 and Jude 24. Notice the phrase "He is able" in the last of these texts. This is the real key to security. Believers are to persevere in the faith; they can actually do so only because He is able to preserve them. This twofold aspect of perseverance is seen in Philippians 2:12-13. But note our perseverance in working out our salvation to its ultimate conclusion (like a problem in mathematics) is possible only because God is supernaturally working in us. Likewise in 2 Timothy 2:19 those who claim to be Christians depart from evil (human side) because the Lord knows those who are His (divine side).

> — ✦ —
> **Our perseverance in working out our salvation to its ultimate conclusion is possible only because God is supernaturally working in us.**
> — ✦ —

There are many other passages which teach that once a person is saved he is saved eternally. The very phrase "*eternal* life" would be a contradiction if it were only conditional. Romans 8:31-39 gives four rhetorical questions with the divine answers, all showing that nothing can separate us from God's love. Other verses that may help doubters are: John 6:37, 39; Romans 11:29; 1 Corinthians 1:8-9; Philippians 1:6; and Ephesians 4:30.

True, there are some passages that seem to teach that a person could lose his salvation, but only if these verses are taken out of context. Matthew 24:13 is often used out of its context and misapplied to the church age. The word "saved" is the same as the word "delivered" in Greek. Christ is promising that the Jews who go through the tribulation and endure the onslaughts of the enemy of God's people will be delivered. Their very "hanging on" shows that they have really believed.

Many verses presented against security actually refer to those who only profess to be saved, or to people who have reformed their lives in their own strength—those without divine life. Matthew 13:1-8 gives examples of these who fall because there is no indication of genuine salvation. Holding fast is an evidence of salvation and not a condition of it in 1 Corinthians 15:1-2 and Hebrews 3:6. First Timothy 4:1-2 speaks of apostates—false professors who never were actually born again. Notice that it says "*the* faith," referring to the Christian faith rather than to personal faith in Christ, which apostates do not have. The false teachers in 2 Peter 2:1-22 were "bought" in a provisional way only; it does not say that they were ever actually saved. The fact they are called "dogs" shows that they were unclean outsiders to begin with.

John 15:6 seems to teach (to some) that the branch is removed and *lost*. Actually, Christ is talking to the disciples who are in Christ about *fruit-bearing*—not salvation. The branch is cast out of its place of fruit-bearing if it does not abide in Christ.

Hebrews 6:1-8 is often used to teach that believers can "fall away" from salvation and thus be lost. Such a view is contrary to the whole setting of the book of Hebrews. This epistle was written shortly after the death of Christ to professing believers of Jewish background and it contains some very special exhortations and warnings. It exhorts the believers to leave behind the rituals of Judaism and to mature in the realities of Christ (Heb. 6:1-3). The epistle contains several severe warnings to Jewish people who were falsely professing to be true believers in Christ (Heb. 2:1-3; 3:7-13; 6:4-8; 10:26-31). Such people had been mentally (but not spiritually) "enlightened" with the gospel. Despite such spiritual opportunity, these people chose to reject the blessings of Christ and to return to the dead ritual of Judaism. For such people there was no hope. God offered them everything, but they willfully closed the door of spiritual opportunity upon themselves. After standing at the very threshold of salvation, they decided to reject Christ and thus put Him to an open shame (Heb. 6:6b).

While this passage related to a specific people group at a particular time in history, it does apply to people today who study Christianity and observe God at work around them, only to decide to reject the Savior anyway. To such people God can offer nothing further—only eternal judgment. The passage does not apply to genuine believers in Christ.

Galatians 5:4 speaks of "falling from grace." This means to fall down from the high principle of living by grace to the lower principle of legalism. The idea of "falling" here does not refer to falling from heaven to hell. Other verses such as Colossians 1:21-23, 1 Corinthians 9:27, and John 13:8 are sometimes quoted but these actually speak of loss of *rewards* or *fellowship* for believers.

For a detailed study of assurance and security, see the ECS course *Securely Saved and Sure of It!*

> We did not earn salvation by *merit;* we cannot lose salvation by *demerit.*

The attributes and works of each person of the Trinity guarantee a permanent, sure salvation. The very character of salvation proves eternal security—not only is it of divine origin and related to election for glory, but it is totally by grace. We did not earn salvation by *merit;* we cannot lose salvation by *demerit.* It is finished. God has revealed to us that we have *eternal* life and security as an incentive to worship and praise Him, as an incentive to holy living, and as an incentive to serve Him. Both our souls and our reward for service are secure. We shall "*never* perish"!

6

ECCLESIOLOGY:
THE STUDY OF THE CHURCH
– PART 1 –

While most scholars agree as to what the churches were like in New Testament times, many do not think New Testament church principles are important. In fact, some claim that the scriptural pattern is not "practical" today. However, if God has given us a guide in the New Testament as to how the churches are to be organized and to worship—in general principles, at least—we should obviously follow it.

The Formation of the Church

The word translated "church" in the New Testament means a "called-out group" or "assembly." The term is used of an assembly of pagans at Ephesus (Acts 19:32) and of Israel in the wilderness as a congregation called out of Egypt (Acts 7:38), but most frequently it is used of a group of believers in the Lord Jesus Christ.

In the last sense it is used in three distinct ways today: (1) It is used of all those living, dead, or yet unborn who have believed or will believe in Christ from Pentecost until the rapture. This is the body of Christ, the universal church. (2) It is used to refer to an era, for example, "the 16th century church." (3) It is used of believers in a locality who gather together in the name of the Lord Jesus to worship, pray, study, witness, etc. When several assemblies of Christians are referred to in an area, the plural "churches" is generally used in the Bible, e.g., in Galatia (Gal. 1:2) and Macedonia (2 Cor. 8:1). Note that Scripture never speaks of a *building* where Christians meet as a church. Neither does it speak of an association of churches or of church denominations. These are all modern conceptions.

Pictorial illustrations often clarify an abstract concept, and the Bible is full of such helps. In Ephesians we have several pictures of what the church is in relation to God.

The church is *the body of Christ* (1:22-23). Christ is the Head in heaven, and His people are the members of His body on earth with important functions to perform. See also 1 Corinthians 12:12-13.

It is *a building* (2:20-22). Christ is the Chief Cornerstone of the building, the temple where God dwells. See also 1 Corinthians 3:9, 16.

It is called *a new man* (2:15). From the former factions of Jews and Gentiles, God has made one new man—a new creation, the church.

It is *the bride of Christ* (5:25-27; 2 Cor. 11:2). Here the church is seen as an object of affection. (It is similar to Israel being the wife of Jehovah, though not the same.)

There are other pictures also in other parts of the New Testament, such as a flock (John 10:16, God's field (1 Cor. 3:9), God's house, and the pillar and ground of the truth (1 Tim. 3:15).

Because the church was unknown in Old Testament times, to the point that God "hid" it from the saints of those days, that there would some day be one new body composed of Jew and Gentile, the Bible calls the church a "mystery." This means that it is a sacred secret now made known by God through the New Testament apostles and prophets (see Ephesians 3:4-5, 9; Colossians 1:26; Romans 16:25-26). Christ predicted in Matthew 16:18, "I will build My church" (future tense) and in Acts 1:5 He promised His disciples that they would be baptized with the Holy Spirit. Acts 5:11 speaks of the church as being in existence, and 1 Corinthians 12:13 shows that the body of Christ was formed by the Spirit's baptism.

The event of Pentecost (Acts 2:4) took place between Christ's predictions and the reference to the church in Acts 5 that fits in with Paul's description of the Holy Spirit baptizing all believers into the one body. At Pentecost, they were all "filled with the Holy Spirit." Pentecost, then, is the birthday of the Christian church. Some features of Judaism are retained in Christianity, but as to origin, purpose, and destiny, Israel and the church are quite distinct. To confuse such dissimilar bodies is to confuse much of the special biblical teaching that relates to Christians and to Jews respectively.

This has the effect of watering down the gracious provisions of Christianity with the legalism of Judaism.

The Function of the Church

What means has God established that will make a local church function to be a glorious testimony to His wisdom and grace? He has given His saints power, gifts, organization, the ordinances, discipline, women's ministry, and means of support. We will address some of these in the next chapter.

Power

The **power** of the true church is in a person—none other than the Holy Spirit. "You shall receive power when the Holy Spirit has come upon you" (Acts 1:8). The church was born in a prayer meeting, for that is how the power of the Spirit is obtained—through prayer. In Acts 2:42 we read that the early believers "continued steadfastly in the apostles' teaching and fellowship, in the breaking of bread and *in prayers*" (emphasis added).

The Holy Spirit, and none other, is Christ's Vicar (representative) on earth. His leading should be sought in deciding on public ministry, disbursing funds, arranging services, disciplining wayward believers, and all other things, both great and small. It is comparatively easy to formulate a manmade program, but it takes spiritual leadership to consult and expect an answer from God the Holy Spirit. It is wrong to "quench" the Spirit by fixed regulations that limit His powerful working. As long as things are done "decently and in order" (1 Cor. 14:40) and in the framework of New Testament principles, nothing requires that every local assembly must be exactly like every other one in its services or in other non-essential ways. The leadership of gifted brethren and scripturally recognized elders will keep things in order.

Gifts

When Christ ascended, He gave **gifts** to men. The gifted men were then given to His church to build it up (Eph. 4:8-16). The men are called gifts: apostles and prophets, evangelists, pastors, and teachers. In 1 Corinthians 12:8-10 there is a list of "gifts" which are endowments that the Spirit may bestow on any believer, whether he is a pastor, teacher, or evangelist or not.

It is possible to do the work of an evangelist in pointing one to the Savior without being a full-time evangelist. Here we shall just discuss the gifts of Ephesians 4.

The People Gifts

The **apostles**, in this context, were for the founding of the church (Eph. 2:20). They were witnesses to our Lord's resurrection and had special powers from God. (Paul saw the risen Christ at his conversion on the Damascus Road.) There are no apostles today in the full sense of the term, though all missionaries (the word *apostle* means "sent-one") do similar work—but without the spectacular gifts of Peter and Paul, or their authority. Those who claim apostleship today are merely trying to usurp authority. They are to be avoided. The apostles have no "successors."

Before the New Testament was written, the New Testament **prophets** had direct revelations from God and made predictions that came true; they also spoke before the churches. No one today in the church has direct revelations from God since the completed New Testament gives us all we need for faith and practice. People who claim to be on a level with the New Testament prophets today are either deceived or deceivers, or both.

We always need and always will have **evangelists** in the church. Whether well-known or locally known, these men are not only endowed with the gift of winning men to Christ by proclaiming the gospel but are also responsible to equip believers to share their faith. A true evangelist depends on the Holy Spirit to get people to decide for Christ. Much reproach has been brought on the church by types of "evangelism" that are not scriptural or honest. It is better to have few or no "decisions" than false professions that last only a few months or even less.

Pastors are under-shepherds. Christ is the Chief Shepherd. Pastors (always plural in the New Testament) are gifts, not rulers of local churches, as is so commonly and erroneously thought. Usually they seem to be the same persons as those who have the office of elders or overseers. The pastors are so closely associated in the original text with teachers that many believe they are two aspects of one gift; that is, you cannot be a real pastor unless you have the gift of teaching also. Shepherds certainly do feed the flock with the spiritual food of the Word of God by teaching, but there are other things that pastors should do to help the flocks in which God has set them.

Words of encouragement, visitation of the sick or backsliding, counseling those with problems, are just some of the many things to be done.

A shepherd's heart will tell a man what is needed, with the Holy Spirit's aid. The church that is blessed with several pastors is fortunate indeed, especially if it is a large congregation. For one man to have the responsibility of pastoring hundreds or even thousands is more than should be asked of any man, no matter how competent and sincere.

Everyone knows what **teachers** are—those who impart information. In the spiritual realm a teacher is much more, because the gift of teaching entails living what is taught, and what is taught is the inspired Word of God. The "doctrine" of the apostles (Acts 2:42) is simply the teaching of the apostles. No true teaching takes place on the scriptural level without the Holy Spirit. It is possible to learn facts and even sound doctrine in an academic way, but that merely feeds human pride and hinders spiritual growth.

The ideal place to learn is in the local church from those with the teaching gift. A little is learned at a time, so that it may be put into practice. A formal biblical education in a sound Christian school can be a great help for systematic teaching and for the acquiring of certain background helps that are not taught perhaps in local churches. It is not essential to have formal training before a man can minister in the church; training from the Word is what counts most. Some who have educational prestige do not always have spiritual life—and many churches have been wrecked because of this. We should honor, respect, pray for, and support all those who minister in evangelizing, pastoring, preaching, and teaching.

Organization

What does the New Testament teach about *organization*? God is a God of order. He is "not the author of confusion" (1 Cor. 14:33). In the local church there should be order, but it should be God's order, not man's.

The letter to the church in Philippi was addressed to three classes of people: saints, bishops, and deacons. Saints, that is, the whole congregation, include the bishops (overseers) and deacons, but the latter two are groups with special organizational responsibilities in the local church. There were a number of each group in the congregation in Philippi, which is the order throughout the New Testament. While the "officers" (if we may use that term) are important, the whole body of worshiping priests gets first place in the apostle Paul's greeting, which is much different from some of the systems prevalent today, where the so-called "laity" take second place to the "clergy."

The word **bishop** is simply an anglicized form of a word meaning "overseer" or "superintendent." It does not mean a clergyman with authority over several churches, for scripturally there are several overseers in one church. Acts 20 (compare verse 17 with verse 28) and Titus 1 (compare verse 5 with verse 7) prove the terms "bishop" and "elder" to be synonymous. The difference in terms stresses the *duty* (overseeing) and the *dignity* (elder) of the men holding this position. The biblical qualifications for eldership are high and spiritual. Those who are successful in business do not necessarily qualify as elders. 1 Timothy 3:1-7 and Titus 1:7-9 give clear and detailed qualifications for elders. Only the Holy Spirit can show who is worthy of this high office. He will choose those who will look after the flock like shepherds and not masters, those who can control themselves and their families, and can contend for the faith against false teachers (1 Pet. 5:2; Acts 20:28).

Even though it is the duty of elders to rebuke and exhort the flock—and this may make them unpopular with offenders—we are to esteem them highly (1 Thess. 5:13) and give "double honor" (the word often means financial help) to those who rule well (1 Tim. 5:17). Faithful bishops work hard and will receive "the crown of glory that does not fade away" when the Chief Shepherd comes (1 Pet. 5:4).

The Greek word *diakonos* simply means "servant." Sometimes it is used in a non-technical sense in the New Testament and is so translated. Sometimes it is used in the special sense of Philippians 1:1, and then it is merely anglicized to **deacon**. Acts 6:1-7 is probably the first passage about deacons. The actual word is not used in this passage, but a related verb ("serve") is used. Actually, deacons' service is wider than merely waiting on tables, and probably includes all sorts of work not the direct responsibility of the elders. The requirements for deacons are high (1 Tim. 3:8-13) and are similar to those for elders. Also they must be proved before being allowed to serve (v. 10). Reverence for God, soundness in the faith, and no lust for wealth are some of the requirements. Verse 11 may refer to the deacons' wives, or possibly to deaconesses. Romans 16:1 may refer to Phoebe as a deaconess or simply as a servant in the church in the general sense. Deacons who serve well win a good standing and great confidence in the faith (1 Tim. 3:13).

7

ECCLESIOLOGY: THE STUDY OF THE CHURCH – PART 2–

The Purpose of the Church

Before we go on and consider further aspects of the life and practice of the church, let us address the question of why God formed the church in the first place. Contrary to the teaching of many, God did not institute the church to convert the whole world. A review of Scriptures like 1 Timothy 4:1-3 and 7; 2 Timothy 3; 4:1-4; 2 Peter 2; and Jude 3-4 reveal that the last days will be full of apostasy, not revival.

We find the answer to this question in the book of Ephesians: ". . . to the intent that now the manifold wisdom of God might be made known by the church to the principalities and powers in the heavenly places. . . . To Him be glory in the church by Christ Jesus, to all generations, for ever and ever. Amen" (Eph. 3:10, 21). The church, both universal and local, is to be a witness not only to the world through the preaching of the gospel and the Christ-filled lives of believers; it is also to bear a testimony about God's wisdom to the angelic realm. In the local churches, God receives glory as the believers gather together to worship and praise Him.

Living out God's Purposes

Although Scripture is clear that the world will never embrace Christ and Christianity, it is also clear that all believers bear the responsibility to help spread the Christian faith. This is done through the gifts that each possesses. Numerically and spiritually the church and churches are built up by a chain reaction as pictured in Ephesians 4:12-13. The gifts were given "for the equipping of the saints for the work of ministry, for the edifying of the body of Christ." Gifted leaders seek to mature the saints so that they in turn can build up the body by their service. There is room in local churches for all God's gifts, and unless these gifts are exercised, God and the church are being robbed. The various preaching, teaching, and helping ministries both at home and abroad expand the church, just as they did in the book of Acts. Acts shows how the good news spread from Jerusalem to Rome. It is our duty to spread it to the ends of the earth (Acts 1:8).

———— ❧ ————

There is room in local churches for all God's gifts, and unless these gifts are exercised, God and the church are being robbed.

———— ❧ ————

There is not space here to go into the topic of spiritual gifts, but the student is encouraged to read the main Scriptures that relate to them (Rom. 12:4-8; 1 Cor. 12; 1 Pet. 4:7-11).

But how are we to relate the grand scope of God's purpose for local churches, here and now? We must begin with the principle that each local assembly of believers should mirror the truths of the universal church. These characteristics are

➢ *Unity* Eph. 4:4—there is just one true church
➢ *Submission to the Head* Eph. 5:23 & Col. 1:18; John 14:16, 26—Christ and His divine Representative, the Holy Spirit
➢ *Universality* Acts 2:47; 1 Cor. 12:12-26—all true believers belong to this one body; all believers living clean lives and not holding serious error should be received into the local church since they are in the universal church
➢ *Holiness* 1 Cor. 3:17—God has separated His people from this sinful world as a whole; individuals in local assemblies should live lives of purity and goodness to illustrate this fact and to please Christ
➢ *Growth* Eph. 4:11-12—the church is built up ["edified"] by the gifts Christ has given to His church
➢ *The universal priesthood of believers* 1 Pet. 2:5, 9—this does not mean that all preach, but that all function as worshiping and serving priests

The leadership of a Christ-honoring, Bible believing church, in concord with a submissive congregation, will seek God's guidance as to how these principles work out in practice in their locale and taking into account their individual character and make-up.

Church Ordinances

The dictionary's definition of an *ordinance* is "an authoritative decree or direction; a law set forth by a governmental authority; something ordained or decreed by a deity; or a prescribed practice, or ceremony." Elements of all four of these definitions fit the two practices routinely carried out in Bible believing churches, water baptism and communion.

First, we must acknowledge that people have made many **ordinances** or sacraments, but the Word of God knows of only two, as mentioned above. These ordinances confer no "grace" or favor from God or man upon the participants; rather, they are tokens of love and obedience to the Savior. One major difference between them is that the ordinance of baptism is rightly administered only once, whereas communion may be observed frequently.

> **The ordinance of baptism is rightly administered only once, whereas communion may be observed frequently.**

The Doctrine of Water Baptism

Some make baptism a requirement for local church "membership." While ideally every Christian should be baptized, there is no Scripture linking baptism with church membership. In fact, there is no Scripture about local membership at all. Much controversy about baptism could be eliminated were it generally understood that baptism is an outward sign of what has been accomplished in the heart. Baptism does not wash away sin; it can neither save nor help save.

Some believe that baptism indicates a new start in life, and signifies identification with Christ in His death, burial, and resurrection. Others feel it symbolizes being baptized in the Holy Spirit. All evangelicals agree it is an act of obedience to Christ's command and sets one apart publicly to live a Christian life. In some countries even today baptism of converts rather than simply profession of faith is the signal for persecution by unbelievers.

The word *baptize* comes from a Greek word meaning "to dip," or "submerge." It has a secondary meaning of "identification" and identification with Christ is an important concept in baptism. Immersion is the correct mode of baptism. John the Baptist picked a spot where there was "much water" (John 3:23), which would have been unnecessary if sprinkling or pouring were the mode. Jesus, when He was baptized, went up "out of the water" (Matt. 3:16) and Philip and the Ethiopian eunuch "went down both into the water" (Acts 8:38).

More important than even the meaning or mode of baptism are the subjects of baptism. It is possible for an unsaved but religious person to be baptized in every possible mode by every organized group in Christendom and still be unsaved in God's eyes! The New Testament teaches that only believers are baptized. All those baptized need not be adults, but they must have received Christ. Baptizing babies and others who are not saved gives a false sense of security, since it is so easy for man to put his trust in religious ritual. In Acts, the order is always "believe and be baptized" and never the reverse. The household of the Philippian jailer is sometimes used as proof that whole families should be baptized, regardless of whether they are yet all believers—but he "believed with all his house" (Acts 16:34). Christ has commissioned His followers to go and teach all nations and to baptize new disciples. Let us see that the teaching is scriptural, and also the baptism itself (Matt. 28:19-20).

The Doctrine of Communion

The remembrance of Christ in His death and resurrection is called either "communion," "the Lord's Supper," or, as in Acts, "the breaking of the bread." The communion is a simple rite which, like baptism, is commanded in the Gospels, practiced in Acts, and explained in the Epistles. On the night of His betrayal the Lord Jesus instituted the breaking of bread and the drinking of the cup as a remembrance of Himself in His death until He returned (1 Cor. 11:26). It is important to remember Him in this way, since it was His request. Knowing human weakness, the Savior graciously provided tangible symbols—the bread speaking of His body given for us, and in which He suffered the

> *Communion is commanded in the Gospels, practiced in Acts, and explained in the Epistles.*

hostility of men and the penal judgment of God, and the fruit of the vine speaking of His blood shed for our sins on the cross. These emblems vividly bring to mind the greatest proof of His love for the church.

As believer-priests who have come together to worship the Lord in His death, we portray the unity of the body of Christ and gain direct access to God's presence (Heb. 10:19-22). The communion service has been the central worship of most of the professing church down through the ages. In modern times, some have neglected the Lord's Supper for fear of ritualism; but if the Holy Spirit has liberty to draw out the heart-worship of God's people, there is no need for the breaking of bread to become a mere ritual. A true remembrance meeting is a great spiritual benefit to believers and a bulwark against turning away from the person and work of Christ.

There is no rigid rule about how often we are to celebrate the Lord's Supper, but it seems clear that the early Christians did so the first day of the week—Sunday (Acts 20:7). Evidently the offering was taken at this time because the saints were to set aside their gifts for the first of the week (1 Cor. 16:2). A frequent spiritual recollection of the sufferings of Christ is an important part of our corporate Christian life. For more teaching on this subject, see the booklet *Our Reason To Be,* published by ECS Ministries.

The Doctrine of Disciplining Sinning Believers

It is the duty of the leadership of the church to **discipline** any who lead lives that are immoral or careless, or any who spread false doctrine. Many churches have no discipline at all today for fear of losing members. Also a person may be under discipline in one area or group and then be accepted in another as if nothing were wrong. The whole purpose of discipline is to restore the erring ones to fellowship. Tact and grace are imperative in this, but if the church is to be holy, as God commands, warnings must be made to the "unruly" (1 Thess. 5:14). The "disorderly" are to be avoided (2 Thess. 3:11, 14-15) along with those who sow discord (Rom. 16:17), and heretics are to be flatly rejected (Titus 3:10). A heretic in the New Testament is one who causes division by embracing false views on important doctrinal matters. The final form of discipline is excommunication (1 Cor. 5:11, 13). This should be done gravely, and should extend to the kinds of sinning saints listed in that passage.

All discipline should be fair, and church matters should be kept within the confines of the congregation. If some of the totally disqualified persons now claiming fellowship in certain otherwise sound congregations were disciplined, perhaps we would see more of God's blessing in the gospel testimony.

The Doctrine of the Role of Women

The **service of women** in the churches is broad and very important, but it is not a pulpit ministry. While spiritually equal to men in Christ Jesus (Gal. 3:28), the women are not to speak in church meetings (1 Cor. 14:34-35) or to teach or usurp authority over the men (1 Tim. 2:12). She may still teach other women and children, but not groups that include men. Women are to wear a head covering as a sign of submission to the man and as a testimony to the angelic hosts which observe the church's order (1 Cor. 11:10). The reason for women's submission is that woman was second in creation but first in the fall.

If a woman cannot be a preacher, public teacher, or elder, what can she do? She can serve God with her material goods (Luke 8:3), she can practice hospitality (Rom. 16:1), and she can teach younger women (Titus 2:4). She can even help teach men in an informal way outside the church, as Priscilla helped her husband Aquila to teach Apollos (Acts 18:26). She can be an encouragement to all. Devout women have been active in charity, foreign missions, and innumerable other service over the centuries. Women can easily stay within the bounds of Scripture and yet never lack for service to Christ and the church.

The Doctrine of Financial Giving

Finally, and very briefly, it costs **money** to provide a meeting place for the local church and to support missionaries, elders, widows, the poor, preachers, and evangelists. Where does it all come from? It should come only from believers who give from a motive of liberality and love. Israel was required under law to give a tenth—surely Christians under grace should do at least as well! Giving is to be proportionate to income (1 Cor. 16:2), secret (Matt. 6:1-4), and cheerful (2 Cor. 9:7). We should all give as much as we can because God has given so liberally to us. Let us not forget *His* indescribable gift (2 Cor. 9:15)!

8

ESCHATOLOGY:
THE STUDY OF FUTURE EVENTS

The salvation that God offers man is past, present, and future. Even though the Holy Spirit is constantly delivering the believer from the power of sin, the old nature still remains. The most mature saint has an inward impulse to sin at times. The good news is that the old nature will be forever taken away when Jesus comes again (1 Cor. 15:49-51).

The Old Testament prophesied that the Messiah would come into the world. Some passages said that He would suffer (Psalms 22 and 69, for example), while others told of His glory (Psalms 2 and 72). The prophets wondered how both could be true (1 Pet. 1:10-11). The explanation is that Christ came and suffered at His first advent and will come again in glory at His second advent. Many Old Testament verses tell of Christ's return. Peter and Paul and John all tell us many times that Christ is coming back. Jesus Himself said, "If [Since] I go . . . I will come again" (John 14:3).

A closer study of the passages on the second coming of Christ reveals another fact. Just as the first coming was in two phases, so there are two aspects to the second coming. With regard to Christ's first coming, one prophet said that He would come to Bethlehem (Micah 5:2) and another said that He would come to Jerusalem, riding on an ass (Zech. 9:9). Both of these were literally fulfilled (Matt. 2:1; 21:1-11). With regard to the second coming, some verses speak of His coming *for* His saints (John 14:3), while others speak of His coming *with* His saints (1 Thess. 3:13). Thus, there must be a time lapse between the two advents. We shall consider coming events in their chronological order.

The Rapture of the Church

When Christ returns for His saints, they will be caught up into the air. This is called the *rapture*. The word "rapture" does not occur in our English Bible, but it comes from a word meaning "to snatch away"—used in the Latin translation of 1 Thessalonians 4:17—"We . . . shall be caught up . . . to meet the Lord in the air."

The truth of the rapture is not taught in the Old Testament, since it has to do only with the Christian church, which was a "mystery" hidden from Israel (Eph. 3:2-7). Paul also speaks of the rapture as a mystery (1 Cor. 15:51). He received this truth "by the word of the Lord," that is, by direct revelation (1 Thess. 4:15). Throughout the Bible we read of Christ's coming in glory. The apostle Paul elaborated on this truth by revealing that He would come first of all for His saints.

The two great sections on this truth are found in 1 Corinthians 15:51-56 and 1 Thessalonians 4:13-18. From these we learn that the Lord will descend with a shout; believers already dead will rise first from the dead; living believers will be changed and given a new body; they will be caught up into the air and all this will be sudden, "in the twinkling of an eye."

> The Lord wants us to be ready and watching for Him at all times.

When will this take place? The Lord wants us to be ready and watching for Him at all times—thus no dates are given. For those who love the Lord, the promise of His imminent return is a glad and wonderful "blessed hope" (Titus 2:13). However, along with this is the sobering thought that every one of us shall give account of himself to God (Rom. 14:12).

The Judgment Seat of Christ

"We must all appear before the judgment seat of Christ" (2 Cor. 5:10). Believers will not be judged for their sins at this event because "there is therefore now no condemnation to those who are in Christ Jesus" (Rom. 8:1). At the judgment seat of Christ, rewards will be

> If more Christians lived in the light of the rapture and the judgement seat of Christ, there would be some great changes in lives!

given to believers for faithful, sacrificial service, but some will see with sorrow their works go up in flame, though they themselves will be saved (1 Cor. 3:13-15). If more Christians lived in the light of the rapture and the judgment seat of Christ, there would be some great changes in lives!

The Marriage Supper of the Lamb

When rewards for faithful service have been given, the marriage supper of the Lamb will take place (Rev. 19:1-8). The Lord and His own will enter into inexpressible joy. Details are not given in Scripture, but the marriage supper is an appropriate way to introduce us to an eternity of bliss with the Lord Jesus Christ.

The Great Tribulation

Ever since sin came into the world, man has experienced sorrow and trouble. Earthquakes, storms, famines, and epidemics are the common experience of mankind, and wars have caused the death of millions throughout history. But the Bible speaks of the *great* tribulation (Rev. 7:14). In Matthew 24 Jesus taught about a coming period of trouble known as "the beginning of sorrows." This will be followed by the greatest tribulation the world has ever known (Matt. 24:8, 21). Many more details are given in pictorial, apocalyptic form in Revelation 6-18. Perhaps it will begin as an attack on those Jews who refuse to bow the knee to any image, and then spread to all Jews. God will punish the Jewish nation for crucifying His Son, and so will allow them to be persecuted. But, as so often, Jew-hating Gentiles will go too far, and the wrath of God will for this and other reasons be poured out on the nations as well. At first men will be filled with fear (Rev. 6:15-17), but they will nevertheless refuse to turn to God in repentance. "They did not repent . . . [they] blasphemed the name of God" (Rev. 9:20-21; 16:9, 11).

We may see here, in the grand scope of God's purposes, the main reason for the tribulation. God has always been merciful to man, yet man goes on in sin. Some might say, "If God would punish man for his sin while he is still living, man would know that God is angry and would turn to God in repentance." However, even when God shows His wrath in the fullest way, man does not repent. The great tribulation proves this.

The great tribulation will come *after* the church is taken away (Revelation 3:10—the original means "kept *from* the hour"), and before Christ returns in glory. It will be so terrible that God in mercy will "shorten the days" (Matt. 24:22). Daniel the prophet spoke of seven years of desolation (Dan. 9:27). The first three and one-half years may be relatively calm and even prosperous, but the last half will be terrifying. True Christians will have been caught up to glory before any of this seven-year period begins. They will be safe with the Lord in glory. Still, God will raise up witnesses to the truth during the tribulation also and many will be converted.

The Second Coming of Christ

The great tribulation will come to a sudden end when Christ appears on earth. "Immediately after the tribulation of those days . . . they will see the Son of Man coming on the clouds of heaven with power and great glory" (Matt. 24:29-30). The pre-tribulation rapture is just one aspect of the total picture of our Lord's second coming. When Christ comes, He will first appear to Israel. They will mourn as they remember how their nation rejected the Messiah (Zech. 12:10). All Gentile opposition to Christ's rule will cease when the Lord appears in victory (Rev. 19:11-21).

The Judgment of the Living Nations

Then the judgment of the living nations will come (Matt. 25:31-46). Gentiles who have shown their faith in God by helping His people, the faithful Jewish remnant, will be admitted to Christ's kingdom. Others will be led away to eternal punishment. When all evil elements have been purged, Christ will set up His earthly kingdom.

> The hope of the Lord's return has always been a great source of comfort to the people of God.

The hope of the Lord's return has always been a great source of comfort to the people of God. Naturally this truth has also been a special target of Satan. Scoffers have always mocked at the idea, and in the latter days their attacks will become more bitter (2 Pet. 3:3-4). Furthermore, many erroneous ideas have been put forth, some dishonoring to the Lord and others based on ignorance of Scripture.

Some say the Lord's coming is fulfilled when He comes into the heart of a man when he believes; others say that Christ comes for the soul when a child of God dies. While there is a measure of truth in these statements, the actual return of Christ is personal, literal, and physical—"This same Jesus . . . will so come in like manner as you saw Him go into heaven" (Acts 1:11). In death, moreover, believers go to Him.

There is a teaching (called the *post-millennial view*) that teaches that this world will become better and better—until the entire world is eventually "Christianized." Two world wars in a single generation surely have not helped the theory that the gospel is gradually improving the world.

Some Christians feel that the church must go through the tribulation, or at least through part of it, in order to be "purged" of its sins. The tribulation thus becomes a kind of a "Protestant purgatory." There *is* chastening for the believer, but it is intended to keep him from continuing in sin. The tribulation is to punish a wicked world for its sins.

> In the wisdom of God, it is better that we should not know the time of Jesus' return. The thought that He may come today will make us want to be prepared.

According to the "partial-rapture" theory, part of the church must go through the tribulation, namely, those believers who are not obeying the Lord in this world. If this were true, part of the body of Christ would be enjoying the marriage supper in glorified, resurrection bodies while the other part on earth would be going through fiery trial. But Christ will not be satisfied until all His own are with Him where He is. Also, what of the many carnal Christians already gone on before? Must they be raised to suffer?

Still others have set dates for the second coming—dates based on everything from a fanciful, mystical interpretation of the numbers and names of the Bible to astrology and even the measurements of the pyramids of Egypt! Such efforts always fail. Even the Son of Man on earth did not claim to know the day nor the hour (Mark 13:32). In the wisdom of God, it is better that we should not know the time of Jesus' return. The thought that He may come today will make us want to be prepared. "Everyone who has this hope in Him purifies himself, just as He is pure" (1 John 3:3).

The Millennium

Old Testament prophecy tells of a golden age in the future when the Messiah will reign as King over the whole earth. In Revelation 20:4 He is seen reigning for a thousand years. This period is called the *millennium*, from two Latin words meaning "a thousand years." The earth was put under a curse because of Adam's sin (Gen. 3:17-18), and the ground now produces thorns and weeds. Paradise will be restored (Rev. 2:7) and the desert will "blossom as the rose" (Isa. 35:1). Wild animals will be tame (Isa. 65:25), and all creation will be delivered from suffering (Rom. 8:19-22).

During the millennium the nations of the world will be prosperous. There will be no war (Isa. 9:7) and crime will be at a minimum. The present enormous drain on nations for police and defense measures even in times of peace will be eliminated. False religions cost millions to keep up their elaborate ritual. In Revelation 17 and 18 we see the end of commercialized religion. A simple spiritual order will suffice in the millennium. Sickness and death will be the exception rather than the rule. People will live to a great age (Isa. 65:20). Those who are spared to enter the millennial kingdom may not be many in number but the world's population will increase, and Christ the King will provide for all. Children born during the millennium will have the opportunity of being born again, and many will be. Even those who do not actually believe will be obliged to maintain outward righteousness (Isa. 11:4-5). Satan will be bound (Rev. 20:2), and no doubt his hosts of evil spirits will also be restrained.

In Isaiah 60:12 we see that Israel will be the leading nation of the world. This place will be given to her by the King of Israel, the Lord Jesus Christ. The twelve apostles will join the Lord Jesus in ruling Israel (Matt. 19:28). Jews who have proved their faithfulness during the tribulation will be given authority too (Luke 19:17). Christians are members of Christ's body, and as His bride they will go wherever He goes (John 14:3).

During the millennium, with Christ on the throne, all people will be forced to obey. But when the opportunity arises many will rebel against the King. At the end of the thousand years Satan will be loosed for a time (Rev. 20:3). He will gather an innumerable army for the last great effort to overthrow the throne of God. This army will all be destroyed by fire from heaven (Rev. 20:9); the devil will be cast into the lake of fire (Rev. 20:10) and all resistance to the reign of God will be over forever.

The Second Resurrection and the Great White Throne

Then will come the Second Resurrection. We have observed that the dead in Christ rise from among the dead at the rapture, before the kingdom is set up but the resurrection of Christ guarantees that all men will rise again (1 Cor. 15:22). Every person will stand before God complete with body, soul, and spirit. Only the unsaved will appear at the great white throne, where the books will be opened and every man judged according to his works. The Lord will sit on the throne as Judge (John 5:22). There is no salvation for those who have rejected Christ in this world; their names are not found in the Lamb's book of life. They are banished to the lake of fire, originally prepared for the devil and his angels (Rev. 20:11-15).

> There is no salvation for those who have rejected Christ in this world; their names are not found in the Lamb's book of life.

What and where is hell? The Lord Jesus gave a terrible description of the feelings of the lost: fear, sorrow, and anger: "Outer darkness . . . weeping . . . gnashing of teeth" (Matt. 22:13; 25:30). The wicked will be like "wandering stars for whom is reserved the blackness of darkness forever" (Jude 13). We do not know where hell is except that it is far from God. Jesus said, "You . . . will die in your sin: where I go you cannot come" (John 8:21).

> We do not know where hell is except that it is far from God.

The Bible does not say much about either heaven or hell. We do read of things that will not be in heaven—sorrow, crying, pain, the curse, death. There will be light there and life and love and glory (Rev. 21:22–22:5).

The Eternal State

Time is like a tiny beach surrounded by an infinite ocean of eternity. We do not know how long time will continue. Before the creation of the world there was a measureless period called eternity. When time ceases to be measured, we will come to the eternity of the future. The word *eternity* means an endless or indefinite period of "time." Paul, Peter, and John all wrote of it. Eternity will never end.

This universe, defiled by sin, will be destroyed by fire, and God will create new heavens and a new earth (2 Pet. 3:10-13). Isaiah says the old will not be remembered (65:17). John had a vision of the new heaven and earth (Rev. 21:1). During the millennial period of the present earth, righteousness will rule (Isa. 32:1), but in the new earth, righteousness will *dwell* (2 Pet. 3:13).

——————— ⊷ ———————

During the millennial period of the present earth, righteousness will rule, but in the new earth, righteousness will *dwell*.

——————— ⊱ ———————

Some people imagine the wicked will be annihilated or, perhaps, be reconciled to God. But the Bible uses the same word "eternal" to describe endless punishment as it does to describe the eternity of God (Rev. 14:11; 15:7). Those who finally reject Christ will be separated from God forever. Their punishment will be as "eternal" as the eternal life of the saved.

The reign of believers will be forever (Rev. 22:5). We will be with Christ (John 17:24). We will be joint-heirs with Christ (Rom. 8:17). We will be like Christ (1 John 3:2). We shall be at His right hand for evermore (Ps. 16:11)!